COMPLETE
TRAININ

CW00471292

**Understand From The Origin,
Finding, Personality, Socialization,
Breeding, Care, Nutrition, Exercise,
Health, Grooming, Love And Others
Inclusive**

GEORGE LINDA

Table of Contents

CHAPTER ONE 4

   CHORKIE 4

   Highlights...6

   Facts You May Not Know About The Chorkie
  8

CHAPTER TWO 11

   History 11

   The Following Clubs Acknowledge Chorkies:
  13

   Before You Accept One Into Your Family:
   Chorkie Puppies 13

   Other Details...14

CHAPTER THREE 17

   Do These Dogs Make Good Family Pets? ...17

   Men And Women 18

   Do Pets Of This Breed Get Along Well?......20

   The Chorkie's Characteristics And
   Intelligence 21

CHAPTER FOUR 24

   What You Should Know Before Owning A
   Chorkie 24

What Size Can They Reach? Full-Grown Chorkie 25

What Are Teacup Chorkies, Exactly?..........25

Chorkie Dog Maintenance Requirements ..26

Haircuts By Chorkie 27

Chihuahua Puppies! When Will You Commit To One? 28

CHAPTER FIVE 30

Training...30

Care 31

Feeding 34

CHAPTER SIX 36

Exercise...36

Health 37

Coat Care And Color 38

Kids And Other Animals 40

Final Reflections...41

THE END..43

CHAPTER ONE

CHORKIE

The Chihuahua and Yorkshire Terrier were crossed to create this relatively recent hybrid designer dog breed. The Chorkie is a little mixed breed that most people would find difficult to resist.

It is said to have been bred for the first time in the 1990s. However, this crossbreed has a personality to match its appearance, so owners can anticipate loads of affection, amusement, and stubbornness as their Chorkie pups mature.

The Chorkie is a mixed toy breed that is extremely active yet, due to its small size, can survive when spending most of its time inside. These dogs obviously like their daily walks and other outside activities, but as long as they are given the opportunity to play and run around, they are able to tolerate a few days of being cooped up indoors.

This is a mixed breed that is obedient and kind and gets along well with kids who are old enough to train them and act as the pack leader. These puppies are excited by youngsters, which can ultimately result in trouble and devastation.

This hybrid dog is also independent, loves to be petted, and gets along well with the rest of the family's pets.

Highlights

Chorkies are canines of mixed breed. Unlike their Chihuahua or Yorkshire Terrier parents, they are not purebred animals.

o Brown, white, silver, blue, and black are the dominant hues of chorkies. Sometimes they have solid-colored coats, while other times they have a variety of hues.

Although it's difficult to say for sure, chorkies often have a minimal shed coat and are hypoallergenic.

Your dog may shed a little bit more if they have more Chihuahua in them.

o The Chorkie is a little dog and is susceptible to injury. Children who are older or people who know how to play with them gently tend to fare better with chorkies.

o Similar to both parent dogs, the Chorkie may experience anxiety when left alone for extended periods of time.

o They don't demand a lot of physical activity. A few quick strolls each day should be plenty, along with several bathroom breaks for their little bladders.

o In general, chorkies get along nicely with other animals. As long as they are not left alone for extended periods of time, they could also appreciate being the only pet in the house.

Facts You May Not Know About The Chorkie

1. You may choose a Chorkie with long or short hair.

You can find both short- and long-haired Chorkies due to the varying hair lengths of their parent breeds. Additionally, if your Chorkie is descended from a Yorkshire Terrier, they will be hypoallergenic; but, if they are descended from a Chihuahua, they won't be.

2. Separation anxiety is common among chorkies.

You and your Chorkie may experience issues if there aren't any other dogs for them to play with when you're gone. If you have to go to work every day and are considering adopting a Chorkie, bear in mind that they don't manage time alone well.

3.Chorkies, while being little canines, behave like giant dogs.

The Chorkie is a little companion/lap dog, however it appears that it didn't get the memo.

They are somewhat brave despite their little stature and like playing with larger dogs.

Although this is cute, if you have a larger dog that is clumsy they could hurt your Chorkie by accident.

Details on Chorkies' mixed dog breed characteristics are included below.

CHAPTER TWO

History

The Yorkshire Terrier breed originates in cheery old England, but the Chihuahua breed is Mexican in origin. The roots of the mixed-breed Chorkie dog, however, are far closer to home and most likely originate from the United States.

Although they could have developed spontaneously over time, the charming and beloved Chorkie wasn't born until the designer breeders started purposefully breeding Chihuahuas with Yorkies in the early 1990s.

Breeders probably opted to combine the two parent breeds to create a little, charming companion dog as other designer dogs started to appear. As the demand for the pup increased, they continued to create Chorkies.

Despite being developed as a designer breed, several Chorkies have ended up in shelters or under the care of rescue organizations. If you feel this mixed breed is the one for you, think about adoption.

Check with your neighborhood animal shelters, search for Chorkie rescues, or contact breed-specific Yorkshire Terrier or Chihuahua rescues since they occasionally assist in finding new homes for mixed breed dogs.

The Following Clubs Acknowledge Chorkies:

o Dog Registry of America o American Canine Hybrid Club o The Designer Dogs Kennel Club o The International Designer Canine Registry o The Designer Breed Registry

Before You Accept One Into Your Family: Chorkie Puppies

Although chorkie puppies are quite active, they also require leisure to prevent overexertion during the day. Obedience training should be a priority for anybody who is thinking about adopting this gorgeous mixed breed since they like being naughty whenever it is feasible.

Although this hybrid breed doesn't need much food, it does need a lot of care.

There are a few other details concerning the Chorkie that you should be aware of.

Other Details

1. They're a Little Mysterious

The history of the Chorkie is not very noteworthy, at least not in reliable records.

This mixed breed is therefore not particularly valued even if it is particularly adorable.

2. They Have a Variety of Colors

Although the coat colors of Chihuahuas and Yorkshire Terriers may be those that their owners would anticipate from birth, crossbreeding between these breeds can produce surprising hues that may surprise (but pleasure) owners.

3. They Need Extensive Grooming

You probably won't see many Chorkies spending a lot of time licking and grooming themselves since they don't keep themselves extremely clean.

As a result, owners should plan to give their Chorkies daily groomings and wash them at least once a month to keep them clean, especially if they spend a lot of time outside.

CHAPTER THREE

Do These Dogs Make Good Family Pets?

The Chorkie is a wonderful family dog, but if you have young children who are still learning to walk, you might want to exercise some caution. The Chorkie is little and affectionate, but extremely lively.

The Chorkie may damage itself or bite the youngster if your child falls on the dog. If your Chorkie aggressively seeks out your youngster to play with them, this may get worse. That makes them an excellent companion for your child, but it also raises the possibility that they may both be injured in an accident.

Men And Women

There are a few things you should be aware of even if there aren't many variations between a male and female Chorkie.

Males might be trickier to housebreak up until they are neutered, while females are trickier to housebreak after they are neutered.

Another distinction is that men often require significantly more care than women do. Although females tend to be a little more independent, all Chorkies, regardless of gender, require a lot of care.

The parent breed they most closely resemble is the main element in determining a dog's size, although males also tend to be a little bit bigger than females.

Although it doesn't explain much of a difference, a man and female with identical DNA can have a difference of an inch in height.

Both male and female Chorkies won't be very big, although females usually are.

Do Pets Of This Breed Get Along Well?

The same way that a Chorkie is a wonderful dog for children, they get along remarkably well with other animals. Their tiny size, though, could be problematic. When around larger puppies, they appear to lose sight of how little they are.

Because of this, your Chorkie may inadvertently injure itself playing with larger dogs. Therefore, if you already have larger pets at home, it's advisable to hold off on obtaining a Chorkie.

But a Chorkie is a fantastic choice and gets along well with other pets in the house if you also have smaller dogs, cats, or other animals.

Finally, remember that early socialization is essential for success, just like with other dogs. While a Chorkie gets along with other animals naturally, an older animal that has never been around animals might get fearful. They may become disruptive as a result, which might generate issues.

The Chorkie's Characteristics And Intelligence

While the Chorkie is kind and affectionate, a playful and vivacious little creature constantly seems to be hiding in the shadows.

When living the good life as the owner of this charming mixed toy breed, a recommended lifestyle pattern to adopt is a balance of play and relaxation.

Given their high intelligence, you should anticipate that chorkies will pick up entertaining activities like fetch soon. However, they may be rather obstinate and easily excited, which can make training more difficult and time-consuming than most owners would prefer.

Nevertheless, any Chorkie may successfully learn how to sit, remain, and heal with dedication and regular practice.

The Chorkie often responds well to praise and seldom need a hard hand to maintain appropriate conduct. The typical requirements for maintaining this mixed breed's obedience are consistent training sessions and a secure living environment.

When it's chilly outdoors, especially, chorkies are ready to cuddle up with their human or animal companions. But this breed also anticipates being able to play and chew throughout the day. Pick up your slippers and magazines, and make sure the house is well-stocked with chew toys so that everyone may enjoy them.

CHAPTER FOUR

What You Should Know Before Owning A Chorkie

The Chorkie is a little mixed breed, occasionally even referred to as a "toy" breed, but its personality is certainly huge.

Fewer Chorkies are found lounging in corners or spending the entire day curled up in front of a fire. They'll often make you laugh, occasionally drive you crazy, and always melt your heart. Here are a few additional details regarding having a Chorkie.

What Size Can They Reach? Full-Grown Chorkie

Dogs of mixed breeds include chorkies. They are a hybrid of the Yorkshire Terrier and the Chihuahua, two of the tiniest canine breeds. Adult Chorkies normally weigh between 8 and 15 pounds and stand between 6 and 9 inches tall, according to PetBreeds. Depending on the size of its parents, chorkies can range in size from greater to smaller.

What Are Teacup Chorkies, Exactly?

According to PetMd, teacup dogs like Chorkie pups often weigh under 5 pounds as adults.

By breeding the runts of each litter, they have been specifically bred to be as little as possible.

In order to create teacup dogs (to satisfy the market's demand), some breeders engage in risky breeding practices that might have negative health effects.

Chorkie Dog Maintenance Requirements

The majority of Chihuahua Yorkie mix dogs shed little and don't need much care.

Brushing and regular bathing will keep the fur neatly untangled.

Haircuts By Chorkie

If a longhaired Chihuahua rather than a shorthair was one of the parents, chorkies are more likely to have exceptionally long hair.

While Chihuahuas can have either short or long hair and do shed, Yorkshire Terriers have long, velvety, non-shedding hair. In order to preserve a young appearance, a Yorkie Chihuahua mix can be treated similarly to a Yorkie, with typically long, maintained hair or the "puppy cut." In order to more accurately resemble a Chihuahua, chorkies can also be maintained in close quarters.

Chihuahua Puppies! When Will You Commit To One?

Pictures of chorkies might cause a serious case of puppy fever. Like any puppy, chorkie puppies require a lot of work. Positive reinforcement and patience are necessary for training. Puppies are full of energy and always want to play.

If you have the time and energy to devote to them, the loving and affectionate Chorkie dog breed might be the ideal addition to your family.

A combination of a Yorkie and a Chihuahua can have a long life and will join your household.

You may want to think about adopting an adult Chorkie if you don't have the time to dedicate to a puppy.

CHAPTER FIVE

Training

Considering how bright a Chorkie is overall, you can teach them a broad variety of skills. A Chorkie is intelligent, but they do have a little bit of a stubborn streak.

This is most obvious while moving in. The Chorkie inherits the extremely difficult housebreaking habits of both Yorkshire Terriers and Chihuahuas.

Consistency and good reinforcement are crucial while training a Chorkie. Despite their stubbornness, Chorkies have a strong desire to please their owners, therefore you should capitalize on this trait when teaching them.

Care

As with other dogs, you should continue to take your Chorkie to the vet on a regular basis to catch any health issues early. Your veterinarian can assist you in creating a schedule of care that will keep your dog healthy.

With smaller breeds, anal gland expression is frequently required as well. Your dog might need to have their anal glands expressed if you notice them "scooting" or dragging their bottom on the ground.

You may either ask for this to be done at a grooming visit or do it yourself.

Though not often, groomers may carry it out automatically. So that this unpleasant chore doesn't get avoided, mention it in advance.

The tear glands of the Chorkie are prone to overactivity, which can result in tear streaks close to their eyes. Tear stains may be greatly reduced by keeping a clean hanky or cloth close by and dabbing them occasionally.

Every day, check their ears for dirt and vermin, and clean them as your veterinarian advises. Before they get too long, trim your dog's nails. This should be done once or twice a month. It shouldn't be making noises against the ground. This is where your groomer can assist.

The preservation of your Chorkie's dental health should be your first priority while providing for their needs.

As little breeds are more likely to have dental problems, you should wash their teeth every day.

You can get instructions from your vet on how to properly brush your dog's teeth. Additionally, dental chews can be quite beneficial.

Feeding

An optimum diet for a tiny, energetic breed like the Chorkie should be created. If you overfeed them, they may put on weight, so keep to a regular feeding schedule and don't leave food out all day. You should also limit the number of goodies you offer your Chorkie.

For this elegant breed, a premium dog food is advised. They require a reliable source of protein, and no breed should be fed inexpensive "filler" dog food.

The Chorkie's nutritional requirements will alter from puppyhood through adulthood and will continue to change into their senior years, just like those of all dogs.

There is much too much variance among individual dogs—including weight, energy, and health—to provide a particular prescription, so you should seek your doctor for advice on your Chorkie's food.

CHAPTER SIX

Exercise

The majority of the time, this adorable little mixed breed gets enough exercise because it likes to run and play. To stimulate their brains and encourage their obedience, Chorkies must go on regular walks.

Although they wouldn't object if they had one, the Chorkie doesn't require a yard to play in. With the aid of a ball for retrieve, a puzzle toy, and a training manual or DVD, exercise time may be accomplished indoors.

Health

The Chihuahua and Yorkshire Terrier, as well as the mixed-breed Chorkie, are susceptible to several of the same ailments. While the majority are normally in good condition, a few may be predisposed to certain ailments, thus it's crucial to maintain proper care and annual veterinarian examinations.

The following are some of the more prevalent health issues that Chorkies experience:

o Skin Issues

o Allergies

o Patellofemoral Luxation

o Hypothyroidism

Coat Care And Color

The coats and colors of chorkies are frequently a combination of those of their Yorkshire Terrier and Chihuahua parents.

Chorkies typically come in shades of brown, white, silver, blue, and black. Sometimes they have solid-colored coats, while other times they have a variety of hues.

The typical coat of a chorkie is light in color, silky, and medium length, and it has distinguishing eyebrows.

Chihuahuas are not hypoallergenic, but Yorkies are. Although it's difficult to say for sure, chorkies often have a minimal shed coat and are hypoallergenic. Your dog may shed a little bit more if they receive more chi.

Despite having a medium to lengthy coat, the Chorkie struggles in extremely low temperatures because of its small size.

They can withstand mild to moderate heat. Of course kids should always have quick and simple access to clean water.

Kids And Other Animals

The Chorkie is a little dog and is susceptible to injury. Adults or older children who know how to play with them softly and approach them calmly tend to get along better with chorkies than younger children. Having said that, the Chorkie may be a wonderful addition to your family for kids who are taught from an early age how to behave around and play with a little dog.

Chorkies typically get along nicely with other home pets and other animals. Keep your dog on a leash if you're out in public since Chorkies can be aggressive against unfamiliar canines. Exercise care and keep an eye out.

As long as they are not left alone for extended periods of time, chorkies like receiving plenty of love and attention as well as being the only pet in the house.

Final Reflections

If you're seeking for a playful, devoted, and social furry family member with whom to spend your life, don't neglect this little mixed dog breed. Although these tiny guys have fierce personalities, they are also kind and inspiring.

They make wonderful pals for older children and will help prevent loneliness for grandmother now that she is living alone. Even while they do need a lot of love, care, and training, the effort you put into taking care of your Chorkie will pay off in the form of a loving, safe pet that your entire family is sure to enjoy.

THE END

Printed in Great Britain
by Amazon